First Printing April 2016

ISBN: 978-0991404827

\* \* \*

\* \* \*

ATTENTION CORPORATIONS, UNIVERSITIES,

COLLEGES, AND PROFESSIONAL

Quantity discounts are available on bulk purchases of

this book for educational or gift purposes contact Pens Up Press.

www.PensUp.com
Harlem, New York

# MULES FIGHT BACK

**40 Activist Poems and Stories
by Kristin Richardson Jordan**

*Kristin Richardson Jordan* (signature)

Published by Pens Up Press

## Table of Contents

On the State of Things
American Tragedy

Ugly
Blind Prayer
13
Asking For It
Sandra Bland
Funny
Confederate Trash
Political Hives
Mother America

On History
American and Non-American Irony

Parts of a Tree
Marriage "Equality"
Pride
What my elders teach me
My Ancestors
This is Sint Maarten/Saint Martin
"Back Then"
Tywanza
Man-Made Disaster
July 4th / American Dream

On Growing

    Memorial Day
    The Least We Can Do (Another Shooting)
    Malcolm Lives
    Mistakes
    Dear Teacher
    Evolving Among Thieves

On Resisting
American Women and the War on Blacks

    Black America
    Glasshouse
    Lost Script
    Food for Thought
    Fear
    Activists Beware
    Leaderful
    Cold
    Make Room
    America's Closet
    When Genocide Turns to War
    Justice is Like Baobab Trees
    The War on Black America
    Our Lives Matter
    Mules Fight Back

e

# ON THE STATE OF THINGS

## American Tragedy

## UGLY

Today riding the subway I saw a woman putting lotion on a little girl sitting next to her. The little girl looked like the woman so I assume they were mother and daughter. The girl was about 5, very petite, dark skinned, and wearing a red and black dress. The mother looked about 35 and started off lotioning the little girl's legs which dangled off the side of the subway seat (they did not reach the floor). The mother then did her daughters arms and lastly her face ending with a dab of lotion on the little girl's lips. I might have thought the whole thing innocent enough, perhaps even sweet, if not for the forceful strokes with which this mother applied the lotion to her daughter. The way she

muttered at a scar on the child's knee. And...the

fact that she called this beautiful little girl "ugly"

several times. She ended by palming the little

girl's hair and mumbling something about it

being "too nappy". This poem is my response...

Ugly comes in bulk so all buyers beware

you can buy it on the corner

you can spray it in your hair

you can dress it up real fancy

but in the end it will be shit

for this "beauty" is real ugly

and for truth

we'll have to flip it

For ugly is not your daughter's lips

or "ashy" face

not nappy hairs, lived in skin and scrapes from

play

ugly is everything from this society that has to

be erased

ugly are these boxes and these hurtful things

we say

For far from 5 year old black girls with slightly

light knees

ugly is the epitome of beauty wrapped up in

white supremacy's needs

for ugly is that air brushed beauty queen

that flawless skin that hot comb

ugly is our comfort with simulated similarity

over letting difference roam

ugly is our love of certain looks

and our love of looks over care

and ugly is looking at your child

and seeing only ugliness there

## Blind Prayer

Interesting how recent calls for peace

Cease to include justice for the Middle East

Say nothing of wars fought for oil

Or billions of lives lost

Off Euro-American soil

Interesting still is that these recent cries

Cease to mourn Black Americans lives

Forget to mention Palestine, Burma, or Egypt

Could it be this "mourning" is somewhat

strategic?

# 13

13 year old adolescent

Black female

headaches for a year + 6 months

seeing a neurologist

headaches worse

worse shortly after sex assault

neurologist said nothing wrong = common migraine

poor school performance = ADHD

transferred to a new school cause

perps @ old school

perps indicted

she's testifying

headaches

next, psycho social problems

next, psychological problems

solution = drugs + therapy?

## Asking For It

They said it was her attitude

Her dress pressed against her thighs

Her hair that announced a yes

Above her accented no

They assumed she aggrandized the details

And was angry at her accidental one night

stands

Just embarrassed about that frat house orgy

That's all

Supposedly

Anyway this was "just the campus talk"

And was – is "no big deal"

I wonder how often it happens

Black woman, white men

I wonder how many can even stand to hear

She was abandoned by cops who

Almost always arrest dark skin

So she never did take the stand to "prove"

She was assaulted

So all around they just talk

About her asking for it

## Sandra Bland

Though some seem to still be asleep

And the police claim they have nothing to hide

Not all of us are (color) blind

We see the lies behind this "suicide"

Believe the stories family and friends tell

We get the way this works all too well

Recognize these stations where violence and

lies dwell

We know Sandra didn't hang herself inside that

cell

## Funny

Funny how we claim to guard peace

When our nuclear program could eat Iran's for

breakfast

When the happiest trigger has been ours


Funny that we can throw out labels like

"terrorist"

When we are

The architects

Of the only atomic bomb attacks in history


Funny that in a sea

Of news radio and TV

So many in the USA have something to say

About Iran

But few have anything to say

About how things got this way

## Confederate Trash

The confederate flag still lingers

Like spoiled food

Some wanted to save it

But it was made from tainted ingredients

And kept out so long that the roaches and flies

it attracted

Made a new home of the countertop

So now it's stain, the smell, and these insects

Still attack our senses

Even as we finally place it in the trash

## Political Hives

If this country were a hive

And we were bees

Then back and forths

Between our two political parties

Would be like fighting over who gets to be

queen

A great distraction for every bee's eye

As they focus on that

and not the slavery of the hive

## Mother America

America is the abusive mother I never should

have had

Way too young to have children

She never really wanted me anyway

Yet here I am outside the womb and taking up

space

Somehow she bore those hours of labor

and nursed me

so as a child I managed not to die

but I still have this suicidal behavior

and I won't forget the times we've fought

and how she beat me, my next of kin

just so selfish, yet still my mother

I am

often ashamed to admit that I

often wonder if I might actually kill her in the

middle of the night

like it was just all wrong from the start

but now it's all stated

and she's right here

and I'm right here

as America still gave birth to me

# ON HISTORY

## American and Non-American Irony

## Parts of a Tree

I wonder how a seed feels before it's free

Wonder if it battles its shell

Before it victoriously breathes

I wonder if the shell then screams when

cracked

Knowing that growth starts with a sprout

But becomes more after that


I wonder if the trunk resents its leaves

cause they twitter and fall

And sway in the breeze

I wonder if then the leaves mock the trunk

For being just so stubborn, so helplessly stuck

But mostly I wonder if a growing tree

Is the home of many inequities

If it's soul is really as hard as rock

If the roots at the bottom are slaves to the top

Is it like the way we do each other?

Hierarchical parts in conflict with one another

Or do all parts of a tree

try to spur growth and live peacefully

## Marriage "Equality"

This is a victory for some of us activists

A crack in discrimination's cage as legality,

legitimacy,

health insurance, and tax benefits get

rearranged

To include something new, a new form of

acceptance

It's a "sad day in America" only according to

Christian terrorists

And yet even as I celebrate I'm also pissed

For this court ruling has not made me equal

It has not stopped the hate crimes the brutality

or the plight of my people

It has not set me fully or even queerly free

For how useful is marriage to those who can't

breathe?

## Pride
*Written in partnership with Xi'an Glynn*

He said I can't believe I'm sitting next to two

lesbians

Made me think of being called dyke,

like when I was outed by a friend on the

playground,

like when my friend's sister said stop hanging

out with that faggot,

like fist fight after fight on a Co-Op City street,

like being cuddled up with my girlfriend and an

on-looker says "that's disgusting."

What was disgusting was his gaze,

that look in his eyes,

us having to ignore him, lie or hide.

June was in full bloom, the season of pride.

But without room to breathe pride surely dies.

With nowhere to go on a moving train

We sat there in silence

Like church prayers

Like decades of days of transgender

remembrance

Like all the hidden and unknown hate crimes

We sat there in silence wanting to hide

Until we found our own courage inside

Unmoved by his ignorance

We made a moment of bliss.

Leaning into each other and sharing a kiss.

He didn't leave us immobile; paralyzed in fear.

We left the train station.

Proud to be queer.

## What my elders teach me

This poem was written in the wake of the Charleston Nine shooting in South Carolina.

me: "I'm very tired"

my mother: "YOU'RE tired. You only just got here...we have to keep pushing"

old saying from my aunt bunny: I'll sleep when I'm dead

African proverb: However long the night may last, there will be a morning


Many older than me have survived decades

of shots fired by those with small minded views

just to hear about 9 more of our people

murdered

in recent news

so I refuse

to be black-and-blue

hopeless or uninspired

when I look up to see those older than me

fired up

and far from tired


So instead of giving up

I will eat skittles

wear hoodies

swim. pray. breathe

and not be afraid

And instead of sitting down

I will stand up, speak, fight

and not be enslaved

## My Ancestors

I dig for those in my family tree

Closeted histories tucked away in the leaves

Pain's buried them deep with longings to forget

And attempts to protect the children

So now in this generation

I dig through these leaves

Fishing for remnants and missing memories

Stories about how my people survived

For there is great strength here tucked inside

my family tree

## This is Sint Maarten/Saint Martin

It's a story marked by conquerors

Foreigners laying claim to "different" shores

Dividing up land for dollars

And power

But unable to conquer the human spirit

Their chaos shaped diversely strong roots

So now there is a blend of local truths

A patchwork language quilted in Dutch in

French in English

Blended with well-seasoned island food

And nourished by families who crowd around 6-

month olds

In the ocean, teaching first strokes like first

steps

Among salt water waves

This is Sint Maarten


French Dutch and Liberation

Mix official and unofficial flags

the sometimes adopted

Bedded with the still imposed symbols of the

curvy path

From whence the island came

And yet there is a bizarre harmony

Among all those with the ears to hear it

A jazzy soulful rhythm outside of lies and

boundaries

What the people call home

This is Saint Martin

## "Back Then"

Back then blacks couldn't be in certain places

at certain times

and even if you stayed in "your place"

there were lynchings

lives lost. slaughter.


and sometimes even cops would kill our people

and even children weren't safe


because back then we weren't seen as human

and even churches would be attacked

unarmed innocents at prayer

killed

back when the world was racist

Oh wait

That's today

## Tywanza

Three months before Tywanza Sanders was

shot he posted a picture wearing a shirt that

said "I Can't Breathe"

showing solidarity with Eric Garner

I wonder just how deeply he knew

that could be him

would be him

he was not one of those "bad" kids

that is not to say that somehow it would be ok

otherwise

but for those who talk backwards

about "thugs" having lives that lead to bullets

and end for a "reason"... just saying

he was not "one of those"

Tywanza studied and worked and wanted to go

into broadcasting, he was quiet warm and

helpful they say

he was only 26

only 26 but of course when the gun went up his

age didn't matter

he stood in front of his aunt and said shoot me

instead but that didn't matter

just received a college degree to further his

dreams but that didn't matter

he could not save himself or his aunt

as his humanity was shot

as he became just another one of the

Charleston Nine

## Man-Made Disaster

In a seismic fault between pollution and poverty

Thousands of Nepalese are the newest

casualties

Unnaturally it was unreinforced brick

And shantytown slums

Rested on fault-lines aligned with corporate

greed

Now landslides cause traffic jams

And displaced families set up tents in a field

opposite

The airport in Kathmandu

Volunteers attempt to clear debris off collapsed

temples

And damaged buildings tilt haphazardly

As our Earth's crust keeps shifting for dollars

While burning gasoline

## July 4th / American Dream

What happens to a dream covered in star

spangled hypocrisy?

One that is presented as freedom

But reeks of slavery


What happens when red and white stripes

They feel like cold steel prison bars


And little white stars mask incredible scars

Like all who died on trail of tears or wounded

knee

To the lies of great slave owner George

Washington and his cherry tree

Fast forward to shouts of "thugs" at brave

Baltimore youth

Now calls of forgiveness for Dylann Roof

So what happens to a dream at war with the

truth?

Does it clamor for more lies to keep it alive?

Claim surrender as it slowly dies?

Fake progress but keep doing what it do?

Or spin in cycles until we make something

new?


Reference

This poem was inspired by "A Dream Deferred" by Langston
Hughes


(c) 2015 Kristin Richardson Jordan

Please share with care and give credit

# ON GROWING

## Memorial Day

I have no interest in a memorial day

Feigned honorable with lies of American pride

No interest in fake declarations of American

freedom

While this nation continues to practice genocide

So instead like 1865

150 years ago

When slaves buried black union soldiers that

died fighting to be free

this memorial poem

is written for our freedom-fighting soldiers

fallen while striving to help our people succeed

Medgar Evers and Patrice Lumumba

Lil' Bobby Hutton and Queen Yaa Asantewaa

and so many others

the bold and the brave

Who have fought for our humanity

Against those wishing to keep us enslaved

## The Least We Can Do (Another Shooting)

After the blood spilt, lies told, bodies bought

and sold

history erased, families displaced

and deaths of those of the wrong skin tone

the least we can do is know

pay attention and remember

I mean the least we can do is mourn

after the bullets on grass, on pavement, in

glass

freedom fighters caught, propaganda

onslaught, cases lost

infamous non-indictments and lessons on how

great the white man is

the least we can do is cry for an end to

injustices

And seriously. the least we can do is count the

slain as slain

and not re-assassinate ghosts by slandering

names

least we can do is see the dirt and recognize

the pain

least we can do is call a spade a spade

But what's the most we can do?

## Malcolm Lives

Though he's dead he's still alive

For his fight didn't end

And his truth cannot die

Caught in the hopes of all of us still fighting to

survive

The beads in my sisters hair and my brother's

pride

He's in the fears of the power hungry

Scared we may actually succeed and thrive

He's in intellectuals' notebooks

Like a soldier's creed

A symbol as well as a man

Compelling us to lead

A truth over fear

An inner voice

over the noise we hear

And did you know also

He's this weird kind of gateway drug

Inducing all who know him

Into revolutionary self-love

A bold Black blotch on America's dream

A cry for the most oppressed with an eye for

the unseen

## Mistakes

I admit I run up on cliffs then have to retreat

But it's because there are these

Lines in the sand

that I just can't see.

Feels like sometimes I touch a stone and it

turns into a leaf

I seek freedom but find locks and keys out of

reach

I mean sometimes it's like damn, can I get a

map?

I try to climb mountains but get trapped in these

cracks

I mean why

Is the land set up like that?

And then of course I have my own cliffs, dark

valleys, and traps

So life's real interesting with all of these

territories

Yet what's funny is that

Despite all

Slowly I'm starting to love even a crack's glory

I'm starting to love riding the valleys and

mountains of my story

And though there are still locks, I love making

my own keys

And appreciating all the skies

Between mistaking rocks for leaves

## Dear Teacher

Most of us spin our wheels

Crash into walls, wallow in self-pity

And wander aimlessly

Wounded by past scars

Past and current slavery

We fear wide open spaces

And waters that show us our own reflection

We would rather sit behind windows

Watching the world through teardrops

Or sighs

Most of us are barely alive

We will ourselves shut

But not you

You are not like most of us

You bask in water and open spaces

You are genuinely unafraid

And I like that


So I've started to copy

Started to learn about

whole oceans I never knew about


Started to believe I could

That we could

Find ourselves human and whole

And be more than downtrodden

Doing more than staying Black

and dying

Thank you for teaching me

that wonderful secret

## Evolving among thieves

There are some who can't let go of the old you

Saying you are what you did way back when


They like to talk about what you used to do

and don't care that what you know now

is not what you knew then


See some can't accept what's new

They're too busy trying to steal

Your power to choose


Too busy creating new ways

to cast the same old blame

Yet whether we're willing or not

We all experience change

So never mind their resistance

Just evolve anyway

# On Resisting

# American Women and the War on Blacks

## Black America

We were born in jail

But we were born to be free

And the irony of our struggle will haunt America


We were born in jail

But we were born to be free

And the agony of our struggle will taunt

America


And we

Trapped within her borders

Her past history

Duped by white supremacy

we love America

like women who stay

we love in the dream

we sacrifice our own

for thug America


to really be free

we'll have to some extent leave

re-birth our own

and let go

the myth of one America


(c) 2015 Kristin Richardson Jordan

Please share with care and give credit

## Glasshouse

Glasshouse (definition): A place, position or situation involving intense scrutiny.

"Smile, sexy"

"C'mon smile, baby"

"Bitch!"

I didn't smile for you

So now I'm a "Bitch"?

Is that it?

I was thinking of our people locked in jail cells

and on death rows

Our bodies male and female, strung up in

various modern day lassos.

Your speaking to me was too close to the last

time I was catcalled and also

for some reason I don't know you seem to feel

entitled to control the emotions I show.

Yet in any case you harassed me for the next

half a block, tease and taunt and then openly

mock.

But you know what's even more insidious

Than this?

The story I just told will be used by white

supremacists

Another way to control

Black people's power

Another reason to impose frisks and patrol

towers

Like in Baltimore, where that poor mother's

pain

Was used to justify the insane

For beating that Black boy played right into their

game

And no one's focused on why he was about to

throw -

because we don't talk about the bullets.

We only talk about the rocks.

Vilify those who fight for peace

But ignore the police shots

That's why this house is glass

Where I deal with being this "Bitch"

In this home for the enslaved

where truth always comes with a twist

Where white racists would have me stab my

own brother trying to be free

Cause our Black bodies are policed by

genocidal authorities

This house where we kill the brave, use the

hungry, and then blame Black youth.

Where we've been stolen from for centuries but

somehow we "loot"

Where intersecting race and gender just seems

to be too much truth.

This. House. Where. We're. Enslaved.

This land full of greed

Guess I'll have to deal with being a "Bitch"

By helping bring this house to its knees

## Lost Script

He wrinkles his nose and shakes his head

clearly confused at something I've said

Then it dawns on him that I just don't know best

like I haven't yet learned how to pass society's

test

For clearly I'm not his type of lady

Lip a little too bold, thoughts a bit too crazy

So calmly he explains to me what this world is

about

But of course I know the script, it's just that I've

thrown it out

## Food for Thought

There once was a lady who went out with her friends and none of them were served. They got drinks from the bar and had fun and all but their waiter said not a word. The bartender was cool so they stopped waiting for food and got full on bar snacks instead. They did not get bogged down in who was around but just drank, ate and went to bed. The next week the lady went back and saw protestors all in a line. "They don't serve blacks," one protestor said and the lady thought back to last time. You would think she would join the line, right? But she said no, this was not her type of fight. Was she wrong? Perhaps inherently not. I mean after all how many hours do each of us got?

And of course there are times we all trade bar

snack for food, times we work around or aside

that which is rude. Or perhaps we should just

make our own restaurants? I mean there's a lot

of shoulds, woulds, coulds, and oughts. Still the

way she glared at the signs was kinda crazy.

As if the protestors were the ones denying food

to the lady.

## Fear

I'm not scared of the last

"dangerous" neighborhood

Featured on the nightly news

I don't fear same sex couples, communists or

homeless men

so-called terrorists

Nor "foreigners" on "our shores"

not afraid of the drug war

So much as I fear thugs in blue

And I'm neither worried about

nor glued

to what celebs do

don't have time for pettiness

I am afraid we won't make it

That somehow the freedom songs and poems

won't be enough


That even after all sorts of freedom fighting

there's just still too much stuff


I fear this world's impact on little ones

the lies we tell on those who don't fit in


I'm afraid of how we keep defining and

redefining human

to keep someone else out

I worry about

fear and fear-baiting and

how we

encage our brains

fear the way we cast blame

And fear more of the same

## Activists Beware

This poem is dedicated to all those arrested and all those affected by police violence during the NYC for Baltimore protest.

I've seen freedom movement

In jail

Stifled by barricades to silence

Intimidated into a parade

And when that didn't work

violence

I've seen a woman pulled by her hair

And three cops on one man

I've seen marchers with no air

Choked by police copters and vans

In an honest world we'd call it an NYPD riot

But you gotta look deep to see past all that anti-

black bias

For this is what happens when we twist up and

reverse truths

Make the firsts into heroes and the lasts into

brutes

So now justice is parted by a red sea of police

For blue uniforms lawfully shove people down

in the streets

So activists beware

Your peace signs are outdated

Your movement will be corralled into orange

nets while

being intimidated by riot gear and bullet proof

vests

Activists beware

Peace signs are outdated

For police will disturb the peace

Assault and battery your body

Use conspiracy to cover it up and then

Blame

their use of violence

on you

Activists take care

For what they will say is

You broke the law and cops did exactly what

they were meant to do

Still. Please. Let's do whatever we can

Cause change doesn't come without a

fight

for something new

**Leaderful**


We lost some Martins and some Malcolms to

the jails

Had our Nat Turners killed on site

Our Ida Bs face censorship

While the smog of the city blocks our Harriet

Tubmans' lights

But

We are still here

Our Idas and Malcolms seeping

Into libraries and community meetings

Piping up on social media and taking to the

streets

Sometimes clashing with police

Or teaching inside jail cells

We are a resistance still growing

In schools and public buses in the minds of

activist mothers

We are reading between mainstream lines

And corporate propaganda

We are at the heart of radical art

And despite all walls and all false starts

We are being made by the second

And growing growing growing

even more effective

**Cold**

Bell Martin Garner and Brown haunt us like

snowflakes

Each unique though none of them new

They're that type of snow that swarms around

you in windy 30 degree temperatures

While you take shallow breaths.

Most are too numb to notice

Still, the cold is relentless.

Built on chilly well-bought degrees

And those meant to be prison fodder.

Politicians who pretend to shiver with fury

And activists who get paid to trend the next

news story

Well-funded attempts to freeze heated unrest

# Most are too numb to protest

There's no exact temperature at which we

freeze to death

It just comes as a slow drowsiness,

numbness before losing consciousness

It's

relatively painless

And so living really is for the painfully bold

For in order to survive you must first feel the

cold

## Make Room

This poem is dedicated to the too often overlooked female victims of police brutality.

I have been to the front lines of police brutality

for the front lines are my hips lips and hair

My skin too

so make room

As white supremacy has spread my thighs it

creeps up my insides

And I vomit

for I am the one left behind

also the one in the streets

And lest we forget

Also killed

My female body riddled with Rekia Boyd,

Tyisha Miller, Tarika Wilson, Aiyana Stanley-

Jones, Yvette Smith, Eleanor Bumpurs and

other

Black-seeking bullets we just don't hear about.

So make room in your papers, poems, blogs,

testimonials, teach-ins, protests, plays,

documentary videos, and Facebook posts.

Make room for my story.

**America's Closet**

I started looking in my county's closet and

found all types of debris. Along with oppression

and violence of every shape and degree. Plus

skeletons as deep as the eye can see and dust

all around like you wouldn't believe.

I found Mumia and Assata in the closet

Songbirds in cages that ought to be set free

from the closet

I found well-bought school degrees in the closet

And employee manuals to serve corporate

needs in the closet

I found a white Adam and Eve in the closet

I also found broken skeletons that looked like

me in the closet

And statues to genocide's glories in the closet

Found both old and new whips and chains in

the closet

And commendations to rapists in the closet

I've also found laws to oppress and detain the

free in the closet

When I look in our closet people criticize me

because what's in our closet isn't meant to be

seen. And many would rather pretend that it's

clean. Just close that door and busy their eyes

with a dream.

But just how much closet space can one nation

get? We're so busy ignoring the mess that we

ain't touched it yet. We can claim we're perfect

but what does that lie bring? At some point,

some day we'll need to clean out this thing.


(c) Kristin Richardson Jordan

Please share with care and give credit

## When Genocide Turns to War

What happens when freedom is no longer up

for debate?

When spines are stricken from bodies in a

country consumed by hate

When death after death means even the patient

can't wait

When centuries of an undeclared state of

emergency means there's just no escape

What happens after breathing becomes a

privilege?

And the future is you're going to die anyway

What happens after legislative lies picket signs

and poetry lines to white racism

What happens after justice just has no more to

say


What happens when genocide has your back to

the wall?

a gun in your face

after you've been beaten thus far

At some point would you not turn to war?

Would you not try to defend

who you are?


But when those in charge face the

people's power

They justify, excuse, vilify and scowl

Act like all Blacks ought to be "like King"

Scream for all protest to be "peaceful"

And don't change a thing

So think before you blame

Before you criticize

Before you buy the police's party line and the

media's lies

Before you call our Black bodies "animals"

"thugs" "looters"

Before assuming we should die in vain and

never shoot the shooters

Before you throw dirt on people fighting for their

lives

Recognize. We're facing genocide.

And this unnatural problem,

It will scream for solution.

For there will be more and more unrest,

Till we're treated as human

## Justice is Like Baobab Trees

Baobab trees are known for their swollen stems

their ability to hold gallons of water

their ancestral connection spiritually

And their vitamin C rich fruit called 'cream of

tartar'

They live for thousands of years and share all

that they've got

with other plants animals and human beings

Justice is like baobab trees

its fruits feed revolutionaries

and it's strikingly beautiful

even when there're no leaves

rationally, justice always holds water

emotionally, it shades truth

and the strength that taught her

And Lovingly, it's just a sturdy beast

with a trunk dozens of meters high

and a width perpetually deep

## The War on Black America

You can sometimes bribe people but you can't

buy the people's power

You can pay for backs and hands but can't rent

a soul by the hour

See hearts and minds, they belong to their own

master

So all attempts by the power hungry

Will eventually end in disaster

For low wage security workers

They won't always protect the wealthy

As we won't always hold allegiance

To a government that's unhealthy

For it is only when only time only how we

awake

It is not if or why so make no mistake

No matter the hospitals, broke schools, or jails

my people go through

No matter the rapes, homelessness, or what

the cops do

No matter the deeply self-hating and self-

defeating places we've been

At the end of this war... we win

(c) Kristin Richardson Jordan

Please share with care and give credit

## Our Lives Matter

Martin Garner Brown Boyd Bland Jones

Smith Ferguson McKinney Baltimore

Chicago

I feel the need to slow down these names

These stories that shoot like bullets in quick

succession

through our social media streams like the

late(st) Sandra Bland

This hate shoots first shoots to kill and

plays cover up later.

It comes disguised as suicide and drops

lies. Or excuses

I feel the need to slow down these names

and this hate

but can't

It is sharply ripping through us

And yet

I still see hope

I find my family in these ruins and we talk,

share and feel

siting with loss after loss

We still plan our liberation

Rebellious and still alive

knowing our lives matter

(c) Kristin Richardson Jordan

Please share with care and give credit

## Mules Fight Back

I've heard the Black woman's "lazy"

the Black woman's "mean"

just this crazy "Emasculator" or a "baby

machine"

A "hoochie mama" or a gluttonous mess

My body is nonsexual, oversexed or "sassy" at

best

And I've also been called stupid, emotional,

unclean

I've even been judged

by those who call me their "queen"

then worked like a beast

but am stuck outside America's dream

Just trapped and attacked then labeled as

"mean"

But I am still here and I still demand to be seen

See I survive all

I victoriously breathe

And those who think me their burden or feign

me their daughter

Don't know that I'm far from helpless

I. am. impossible to slaughter

I am neither a "ho" nor a "bitch" nor a

"foreigner"

And though cops may kill me

I'm far more than just victim or mourner

See I am that place where gendered race

meets

the principled argument

the shouts from the streets

Put me down, cover me over

I boil up from beneath. And you can't trap the

fire

or turn down the heat.

Being pretty soft spoken, so some mistake me

for weak

But look a bit closer I'm actually a beast

And Angelou's right. I'm the song of the slave

As from Aba riots to Ferguson. I'm shamelessly

brave

I have that Shakur-Hamer spirit. That's why I'm

far from afraid

And once more I'm human. And I won't be

enslaved.


References:

The title of this poem is in reference to Zora Neale Hurston's

novel Their Eyes Were Watching God (Hurston, 14).

References to "The White Man's Burden" by Rudyard Kipling

and "Still I Rise" by Maya Angelou are in this text. Name

references include "Angelou"(Maya Angelou), "Shakur"

(Assata Shakur), and "Hamer" (Fannie Lou Hamer). "Aba

riots" refers to the Igbo "Women's War" of 1929 and

"Ferguson" refers to woman-led resistance efforts in

response to the murder of Mike Brown in Ferguson, MO

2014.

# Acknowledgements

I would like to thank my editors who are also my family. My god mothers Paris and Eshey Harris, my mother Lynne Richardson, and my fiancée Xi'an Glynn. Thank you for taking the time to read this book before it was a book and thank you for all of your time, love, support, and feedback always.

Special thanks to my father Desmond Jordan, my sister Lauren Jordan, my aunt Ellen Jordan Evans, my grandparents Thelma and Victor Jordan and many other family members, and many dear and loving friends. You are always there for me and with me in every adventure. Please forgive me for not mentioning you all by name. Please know that even if you are not mentioned above your love and support matter more than you know and I am forever grateful.

Among my friends, special thanks to my comrades and particularly Justice Hampton for participating in this books launch.

I would also like to thank my teachers and my students. Among my teachers, special thanks to my high school mentor Lavern McDonald at The Calhoun School, to my college professor Corey D.B. Walker, and to the Africana Studies department at Brown University. Among my students special thanks to those at Girl Be Heard and particularly Larissa Jeanniton, Dinae Alize, Jordan "Jay" Delise Fleming and Laura Richmond for performing with me at this book launch.

Lastly but absolutely not least, a world of thanks to Sisters Uptown Bookstore and Freedom Hall in Harlem, New York. Thank you for taking a chance on this book.

Made in the USA
Middletown, DE
29 September 2021

48712032R00066